# Asking the Right Questions

# Praise for
## *Asking the Right Questions*

"Margaret Wheatley once stated that 'real change begins with the simple act of people talking about what they care about.' Although she talked about how change happens in business, the idea is relevant to how real change happens in education. This new book—much needed and long overdue—is a perfect example. It offers a thoughtful and compelling vision for ways educational leaders can facilitate real change. Specifically, it describes a new vision of what educational leadership can be and how it can use stakeholder input to promote continuous district-wide improvement. It is based on sound theoretical principles: educational leadership is proactive and collaborative, it values the voices of all stakeholders, and it recognizes reflection and feedback as critical to the process of continuous improvement. While theoretically sound, this book is also pragmatic and practical. It describes a four-question model of leadership grounded in the notion that the key to school improvement is the process of problem-finding and problem-solving. One way to find and solve the right problems is by asking the right questions. When educational leaders ask the right questions, they create a collaborative, rather than a hierarchical, culture of learning with stakeholders. It is exactly this kind of culture that allows stakeholders (people talking about what they care about) to create a shared vision for real change. I believe this new book should not only be required reading for superintendents and principals currently in the field, but also for students in higher education who aspire to be inspiring educational leaders in the future."

——**William Bintz**, PhD,
professor in the School of Teaching, Learning, and Curriculum Studies, Kent State University

"I have had an opportunity to review the manuscript *Asking the Right Questions: A Guide to Continuous Improvement with Stakeholder Input* and found it to be a tool school personnel can utilize to focus on continuous school improvement. I have been involved with school improvement for over forty years, as a high school principal and educational consultant. In my experience, I have found it is extremely important that school district leaders be involved in the initial stage of school improvement. This book outlining the four-question model by Gay Burden and Stu Silberman, checks all the boxes for systemic change resulting from a school improvement initiative. The four question model helps a leader to collect and establish a collective vision. From my experience central office personnel, principals, teacher leaders, parents, students, and community leaders will be challenged and have ownership in the process after being exposed to the model. I would recommend this book as one of the resources for districts to read, and contemplate using when planning a school improvement initiative."

—**William O'Neal**, school improvement consultant, Southern Regional Educational Board

"I have long been a believer in the simple phrase, 'nobody washes their rental car.' This truth occurs because people do not own it. The same is true with school improvement. Too often the improvement ideas come from outside, garnering little ownership. The process detailed in this book provides schools and districts with tools to engage teachers, leaders and staff members in taking ownership of both the problems and solutions to problems. By focusing on asking the right questions to extend learning and understanding the root causes of both successes and problems, all staff in a district own the improvement efforts. These four guiding questions create a district framework for continuous improvement."

—**Scott Warren**, Southern Regional Education Board, director of Making Schools Work

"There is nothing quite as exciting as being hired as principal or superintendent. Finally, you have the opportunity to put all you have learned—and your many ideas—into practice. But, where do you begin? As any good leader knows, you cannot simply go into a school or district and think that magically, everyone will want to follow a vision that you cast. That vision has to be formed collectively, but how? As a superintendent, I was so fortunate to have a mentor, Stu Silberman, who modeled a very clear process for me. I'd been able to see firsthand the power of listening, and sharing those insights in an effective way. Having a protocol to use for gathering information and feedback was invaluable. It provided me the chance to learn about the district and the people inside, and gave me critically important thoughts about how to best move forward. Having a book now to capture the advice of such talented, knowledgeable and proven leaders is a true gift to leaders everywhere. The advice is practical, straightforward and if you follow it, will ensure your success. This is one you will want to keep close and refer to time and time again."

—**Carmen Coleman**, chief academic officer,
Jefferson County Public Schools (Largest District in KY),
Louisville, Kentucky

"For someone that led two school districts as a superintendent and now works to prepare and support future education leaders, reading Stu and Gay's book provides a refreshing reminder that it is up to each of us to be open, transparent leaders in order to foster a shared vision that will endear all constituents to your school and district, ensure an efficient workplace, enjoin others to help us, enlighten our naysayers, enlarge our opportunities to grow and serve, and ultimately enhance student achievement. It should be required reading for all educators."

—**Tom Shelton**, National Director for District Leadership at
the National Center for Education and the Economy;
2011 Kentucky Superintendent of the Year;
Former Executive Director of the Kentucky Association of
School Superintendents;
and former Professor of Educational Leadership at Eastern
Kentucky University

"This book is a must-read for school and district leaders and those aspiring to be future leaders. While simplistic in form, gaining key stakeholder input using the techniques this book prescribes, literally establishes a powerful force towards school improvement and most importantly, student achievement. Listening to staff, students, and your community is a critical variable for an effective school leader and when coupled with shared-decision making, the table is set for success. Personally, I have utilized these skills as a leader and have witnessed the power in action when you incorporate this key data into a plan of action to fulfill the needs addressed by the various school stakeholders. We have witnessed a cultural difference take place in our school district by simply listening to our people, collecting the data, and developing an action plan to address the strengths, weaknesses, opportunities, and threats shared with us by our own people."

—**J. Matthew Robbins**, superintendent,
Daviess County Public Schools, Kentucky

# Asking the Right Questions

## *A Guide to Continuous Improvement with Stakeholder Input*

Stu Silberman and Gay Burden

ROWMAN & LITTLEFIELD
Lanham • Boulder • New York • London

Published by Rowman & Littlefield
An imprint of The Rowman & Littlefield Publishing Group, Inc.
4501 Forbes Boulevard, Suite 200, Lanham, Maryland 20706
www.rowman.com

6 Tinworth Street, London SE11 5AL

Copyright © 2020 by Stu Silberman and Gay Burden

*All rights reserved.* No part of this book may be reproduced in any form or by any electronic or mechanical means, including information storage and retrieval systems, without written permission from the publisher, except by a reviewer who may quote passages in a review.

British Library Cataloguing in Publication Information Available

**Library of Congress Cataloging-in-Publication Data**
ISBN 978-1-4758-5257-8 (cloth)
ISBN 978-1-4758-5258-5 (paper)
ISBN 978-1-4758-5259-2 (electronic)

# Contents

| | | |
|---|---|---|
| Foreword | | xi |
| Preface | | xv |
| Introduction | | 1 |
| 1 | Four-Question Model Overview | 7 |
| 2 | What Is Working? Things You Do Not Want to Change | 17 |
| 3 | What Needs to Be Changed to Make This a Better Place for Kids? | 29 |
| 4 | What Needs to Be Changed to Make This a Better Place for Adults? | 39 |
| 5 | What Can I Do, as Your Leader, to Do a Better Job? | 49 |
| Appendix: Whole-Group Debriefing Strategy | | 65 |
| Works Cited | | 69 |
| About the Authors | | 73 |

# Foreword

In my initial reading of Stu Silberman's and Gay Burden's draft of this book, my attention was captured as I saw these words: engage, build relationships, collective vision, and collective efficacy. Their focus on questions and a process that built those terms into a school district leader's practice led me to a deeper read.

I have always been drawn to Margaret Wheatley's work with organizational leadership. (https://margaretwheatley.com) In *A Simpler Way*, with Myron Kellner-Rogers (1996) she identified three focus points for effective teams that I believe provide a framework for purposeful leadership actions:

- Flow of information throughout the team
- Rich and diverse relationships among the team members and with the broader community
- A common vision that unites the team

I created this visual to illustrate the connection and the payoff of the three elements.

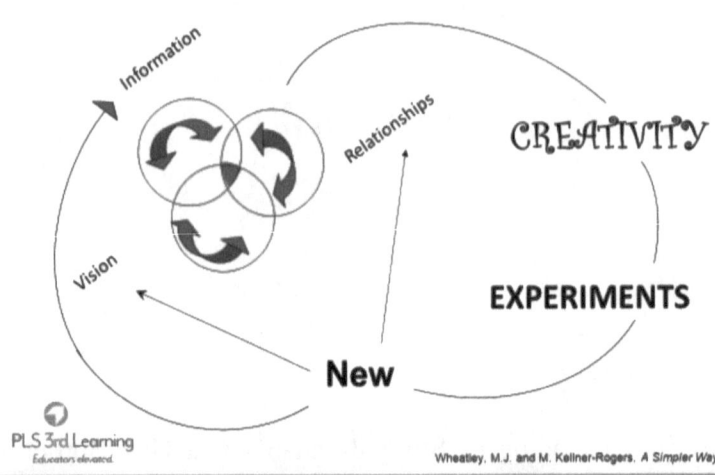

When the three elements of information flow, relationships, and vision are present, the payoff is creativity that produces ideas and possibilities to advance toward the goals of the team. Experimentation and risk-taking with the new ideas produce new information, or new relationships and a tightened or broader vision; pushing the team to continuous improvement or transformation.

The critical four questions that Stu and Gay define and the process of engaging stakeholders in focus groups build the synergy for continuous improvement. They identify a process that has the improvement plan emerge from the very people who are needed to bring about the desired changes. School leaders implementing this plan are modeling empowering teaching and learning behaviors that principals and teachers need to implement in their day-to-day practices. The examples from the authors' experiences implementing the process clarify the value.

The inclusion of the final question," What can I do, as your leader, to do a better job?" encourages district leaders to model the vulnerability that is necessary for relationship trust to be built.

Margaret Wheatley illustrates the problem in *Relationships: The Basic Building Blocks of Life*.

> A simple means to support and develop relationships is to create time to think together as staff. Time to think together has disappeared in most organizations. This loss has devastated relationships and led to increasing distrust and disengagement. Yet when a regular forum exists where staff can share their work challenges, everything improves. People learn from each other, find support, create solutions, and gradually discover new capabilities from this web of trusting relationships.

Stu Silberman and Gay Burden offer a solution. Their process will take real commitment from those implementing it. It will require some risk-taking and the scheduling of the leader's time. The payoff for students is worth every bit of this investment.

Steve Barkley is executive vice president at PLS 3rd Learning. He has provided training, facilitation, and consulting to educators across the USA and internationally for over three decades. His website, www.BarkleyPD.com, provides blogs, podcasts, and videos as resources for individuals and teams.

# Preface

Asking the right questions is not an easy thing for any leader to do. There is an art to asking questions, and there are so many questions to ask. It can be overwhelming for any district leader to know where to start. The Four-Question Model proposed in this book demonstrates how leaders can model connected leadership as they garner input from stakeholders to develop a compelling improvement plan. Far too many leaders grapple with a powerful leadership role that steers the helm of a business or school system. They do not know where to start or change course because they are not asking the right questions.

Connected leadership is fairly simple to define but difficult to put into action. It is easier to micromanage than it is to engage stakeholders and build relationships that lead to a common goal. Because of this, the authors provide a four-question model that any leader can implement with fidelity. Who knew that connected leadership could be made easy with four specific questions? If you are a leader looking for the right questions to ask, this book was written with you in mind.

While the authors draw from their own experience in educational leadership, this four-question model can also be applied to other leadership positions. Since the process is grounded in leadership theory and research, anyone in a leadership or management position can adapt the four-question model to fit their role. The four-question model can assist leaders in developing new or revised business plans, marketing plans, or improvement plans. Educators are not alone in the process of crafting improvement plans, so as you read this book, keep this in mind. Each chapter gives practical educational examples, but you can also reflect on your own examples in your business or industry. Whether you are dealing with employee retention, worker productivity, or workplace culture, this model can promote a collective vision for change. You will quickly learn the value of obtaining feedback from your constituents, clients, customers, patients, etc., as well as how that feedback can be woven into an improvement plan.

There is no better way to model connected leadership in education than to ask important questions, listen to stakeholder answers, and develop a collective plan for district improvement. Once these questions are asked and results are analyzed, district leaders are poised to develop an improvement plan that is more likely to create buy-in from stakeholders. Along with other district quantitative data, the qualitative data provided in this process will garner stakeholder input in the school improvement or turnaround plan. However, in order to create a shared vision, district leaders need to ask stakeholders the right questions.

District leaders often talk about having a shared vision, but they have not found a process to help them reach that goal. In the end, they look for ways to create buy-in "after" the annual improvement plan has been written. What are you currently modeling? Are you a proactive leader or a reactive leader? This process provides a proactive approach that many district leaders can use to craft a shared vision.

We asked educational leaders from across the country what expectations they might have for a book about asking the right questions. One common reaction that was striking was that many of them said this was not an easy question to answer. Most educators grew up in a system that expected students to raise their hand with the right answer. For the first part of our educational experience, even through college, we were focused on giving the right answer—not asking the right question—to make the grade.

As we shifted from the role of student to teacher, we began to focus more on questioning. Effective questioning is when teachers engage students in the learning process by actively composing responses. Through effective questioning we help develop thinking skills, encourage discussion, and stimulate new ideas. In fact, effective questioning is one of the most researched areas in education. Effective questioning is a common measure we use to evaluate teachers across the country. We know that highly effective teachers ask more open-ended questions than less-effective teachers, so we offer professional development on effective questioning techniques and how to ask questions that address higher-order thinking.

Some master the art of questioning, but in many classrooms across the country today, you still see choral responses to low-level questions. The truth is that many of us are not asking the right questions because we have not mastered the art of asking the right questions. Furthermore, most effort in the area of questioning has focused on teachers. Our Four-Question Model can assist district superintendents in increasing their leadership effectiveness.

One former school administrator and national consultant we spoke with noted the questions that get to the "how" and "why" are most definitely the critical questions. Unfortunately, in education, we spend way too much time on the "what" questions. What chapter, what verse, what worksheet, what lab, what text, and so on dominate teacher discussions. How we engage and why we engage in education are far more important.

From the role of teacher, some choose to advance to administrative leadership roles. Administrative preparation programs train us on how to examine data and craft a district improvement plan, but many still do not train us in the mastery of questioning. Let's face it, if teachers do not master the art of questioning, do we really expect them to do a better job of questioning at an administrator level? We asked a professor in the Department of Educational Administration, Leadership, and Research at Western Kentucky University what he thought about a book titled, *Asking the Right Questions*. He said it made him think about "an inquiry-based approach to leadership and school improvement that prompts collective reflection, hypothesizing about strategies, risk-taking, and reviewing of evidence to assess progress—what Professional Learning Communities (PLCs) are ideally supposed to do."

He also spoke about how an inquiry approach stands largely in contrast to some of the more top-down, directive approaches many educational leaders use. The university where he works is currently doing a big revision to their principal program as part of a Wallace Foundation Grant, and cycles of inquiry are going to figure prominently in each class. He went on to say that he sees "asking the right questions" to be essential in this program revision undertaking.

The Four-Question Model outlined in this book help you move beyond the "what" questions to get to the heart of your district's DNA and outline an improvement plan that garners input and buy-in from the front end. If asking the right questions in the classroom is critical to establishing expectations, promoting collaboration, and thinking at a deeper level, then it is all the more urgent for district leaders to ask the right questions. It is an inquiry-based approach that leaders at all levels can use to establish true PLCs.

Being a part of a school district that developed an improvement plan around the Four-Question Model and seeing the positive impact it made on the teaching and learning helped us recognize that this is a model that should be replicated and shared with other district leaders across the country. It is an easily replicable and scalable Four-Question Model that we believe can take the mystery out of the "black box" of school reform.

We would like to acknowledge our family, friends, and colleagues who supported our time and effort in this journey to share the Four-Question Model. We believe this model can help any district leader who believes, "It's about kids!"

# Introduction

To create a shared vision, district leaders need to ask stakeholders the right questions. There is no better way to model connected leadership than to ask important questions, listen to stakeholder answers, and develop a collective plan for district improvement. Once these questions are asked and results are analyzed, district leaders are poised to develop an improvement plan that is more likely to create buy-in from stakeholders. Along with other district quantitative data, the qualitative data provided in this process will garner stakeholder input in the school improvement or turnaround plan.

The Four-Question Model demonstrates how district leaders can model connected leadership as they garner input from stakeholders to develop a compelling district plan. Connected leadership is fairly simple to define but difficult to put into action. It is easier to micromanage than it is to engage stakeholders and build relationships that lead to a common goal.

The whole idea is to create buy-in from stakeholders on the front-end of planning—rather than seeking ways to do so after the fact. "People are motivated by goals which they find personally compelling, as well as challenging but achievable. Having such goals helps people make sense of their work and enables them to find a sense of identity for themselves within their work context" (Leithwood, Seashore Louis, Anderson, Wahlstrom, 2004, p. 8). A Native American proverb says, "Listen to the whispers and you won't have to hear the screams."

The Four-Question Model is framed around these four questions:

1. What is working (i.e., things you do *not* want to change)?
2. What needs to be changed to make this a better place for kids?
3. What needs to be changed to make this a better place for adults?
4. What can I do, as your leader, to do a better job?

As noted earlier, the practical examples in each chapter draw from the authors' educational experiences in implementing the Four-Question Model. If you are leading in another field or industry, you can easily adapt question 2, "What needs to be changed to make this a better place for kids," based on who you serve. For example, "What needs to make this a better place for patients, community members, clients, customers, etc."

We will talk more about the types of focus groups later, but it is important to understand the role different groups play in the district. "A focus on agenda-setting, and the role that different groups play in agenda-setting is warranted because the discussion of key issues and topics affect leader behavior well before any policy is actually in place" (Leithwood et al., 2004,

p. 49). These four questions and specific examples of how they impact district improvement and change are provided by in the following chapters.

The Four-Question Model provides an outline for a connected process that can help successful districts take a new collaborative approach to their district improvement plan, but it can also help districts to shift from a distrustful culture to a culture in which there is more collective efficacy and trust. Once the process is implemented, the organization becomes a better place to learn and work. As Fullan (2001) notes, "Collaborative cultures, which by definition have close relationships, are indeed powerful, but unless they are focusing on the right things they may end up being powerfully wrong" (p. 67).

District leaders often talk about having a shared vision, but they may lack a process of reaching that goal. In the end, they wind up looking for ways to create buy-in after the annual improvement plan has been written. What are you currently modeling? Are you a proactive leader or a reactive leader? This process provides a proactive approach that many district leaders can use to craft a shared vision.

Peter Senge and colleagues (2000) noted that re-creating schools means we must involve every stakeholder in conversations where they have an opportunity to express their aspirations, build their awareness, and develop their capabilities together (p. 5).

To establish a shared vision, Senge et al. (2000) discusses the practice of dialogue. "During the dialogue process, people learn how to think together—not just in the sense of analyzing a shared problem or creating new pieces of shared knowledge but in the sense of occupying a collective sensibility in which the thoughts, emotions, and resulting actions belong not to one individual, but to all of them together" (p. 75). At the end of the process, stakeholders typically start making comments about what a great listener the leader is, building instant credibility.

As the district leader trying to implement change across the system, it's all about relationships, relationships, relationships. Knowledge is power, and "knowledge sharing fuels relationships" (Fullan, 2001, p. 76). Unless you start by determining the district's DNA, you are likely to initiate a continuous-improvement model that may take you in the wrong direction. If the district DNA is toxic or if there are discrete and contradictory strands of DNA, you will often see a community that is polarized, or worse, whole but broken.

If you visit school districts across the country, you can usually sense a school's DNA in the first few minutes on campus. Imagine an Alaskan Athabaskan Village school in Tanana that sits where the Tanana and Yukon rivers meet. The only way in is by dog sled, bush plane, or boat. On your first arrival, the principal asks if you brought any food because the one store in the village was closed because many had gone to another village for a funeral. Teachers typically fly up from the Lower 48 and stay in "teacher trailers" over the winter months. You would quickly learn that the most important part of the Athabaskan subsistence living is sharing. This culture is grounded in the belief that hunters are expected to share with a kin-based network in the community.

Another critical piece of the district's DNA is that many people from interior Alaska are moving to larger cities, such as Fairbanks and Anchorage. However, state law requires a minimum of ten students to keep a school open. Many schools are closing and are being replaced with regional schools.

There is a concern of the potentially devastating impact that closing the school will have on the village community. Can you imagine how different this district's DNA is compared to a district in many other states? Unless you are asking the right questions among stakeholders, you may misread the DNA of a district or school.

Based on your community's political educational environment, you can use the Four-Question Model to shift these opposing factions toward a shared vision. Opposing viewpoints often share a passion around a common topic. This process can help stakeholders focus on what they want to change and actions that can lead to improvement. Once you use this Four-Question Model to determine the district's DNA, then you are poised to craft a continuous-improvement plan that embodies stakeholder input. After all, people really just want to have their voice heard, and they all want what is best for students in the long run.

Leithwood et al. (2004) reviewed the research related to how leadership influences learning, and they state:

> Collegial work groups (e.g., grade level teams, school improvement teams), sharing of expertise, networking of teachers and principals across schools, cross-role leadership and school improvement teams at school and district levels—all these and many other configurations of professional educators collaborating with one another on student achievement-focused district reform initiatives are indicative of a common emphasis on teamwork and professional community as one of the keys to continuous improvement (p. 44).

Too many districts are reluctant to outgrow a "good" system. Just because what you are doing is bringing positive results does not mean that you should become complacent. Complacency is the enemy of urgency, and we can never believe that what we are doing is good enough.

*Chapter One*

# Four-Question Model Overview

### DETERMINING YOUR SCHOOL'S DNA

The Four-Question Model is based on a specific set of questions that can help determine an organization's DNA. When stakeholders are asked these four questions, it provides a space to build the foundation of collective efficacy. Dufour and Marzano (2011) state that we need to, "focus improvement efforts on building the collective capacity of educators to meet the challenges they face" (p. 18).

## Collective Efficacy

The process of creating a collective vision in a district also supports a culture of collective efficacy, which is powerful in impacting student achievement. So, which comes first, a collective vision or collective efficacy? Can they both occur at the same time? Our belief is that one can lead to the other, but you must have both before you will see an impact on student achievement. Collective efficacy has been researched in education for many years. Some of the most powerful data on collective efficacy were reported in the *ASCD Educational Leadership* magazine article by Donohoo, Hattie, and Eells, "The Power of Collective Efficacy" (2018).

The following excerpt summarizes the meta-analysis work on looking at collective efficacy and student achievement.

> Rachel Eells's (2011) meta-analysis of studies related to collective efficacy and achievement in education demonstrated that the beliefs teachers hold about the ability of the school as a whole are "strongly and positively associated with student achievement across subject areas and in multiple locations" (p. 110). On the basis of Eells's research, John Hattie positioned collective efficacy at the top of the list of factors that influence student achievement (Hattie, 2016). According to his Visible Learning research, based on a synthesis of more than 1,500 meta-analyses, collective teacher efficacy is greater than three times more powerful and predictive of student achievement than socioeconomic status. It is more than double the effect of prior achievement and more than triple the effect of home environment and parental involvement. It is also greater than three times more predictive of student achievement than student motivation and concentration, persistence, and engagement (p. 40).

## Stakeholder Focus-Group Meetings

Knowing the right questions to ask is the first step in this Four-Question Model. The next step is to create a schedule of stakeholder or focus-group meetings. These meetings will last approximately one hour each. An individual written survey on the four questions is given at the beginning of the focus-group meeting. Once the individual "anonymously completed" surveys are collected, the questions are used again in a whole-group debriefing strategy called a Think-a-Thon (see the Appendix). You will find that there are great benefits to gain from this highly engaging debriefing strategy.

The process is time and labor intensive, but it will pay huge dividends in the long run. You might be thinking that this is not worth the time required. We encourage you to think of it as a short-term investment for a long-term benefit. This process gives stakeholders a voice in designing the district improvement or turnaround plan. In the end, stakeholders want a platform in which they can express concerns or ideas, and this process provides a setting for that to happen in a nonthreatening way.

Schedule and conduct the meetings with representative focus groups (see suggested list that follows). It is critical that you meet with these groups in person; do not send a delegate. Your visibility in these focus-group meetings is the first step to establishing a shared vision. In their book, *Extreme Ownership: How US Navy Seals Lead and Win*, Willink and Babin address the "Belief" principle. They say that if a leader truly believes in the mission, they will take risks to address any challenges necessary to win. "Actions and words reflect belief with a clear confidence and self-assuredness that is not possible when belief is in doubt" (pp. 76–77).

If you do not attend the focus-group meetings or send a delegate, stakeholders will doubt the importance of the data collected. Presence symbolizes your investment in the process. A career and technical education (CTE) director in a Tennessee school district wondered why the CTE teachers were not buying into the idea that CTE teachers can impact ACT scores.

The CTE director realized that the teachers did not see him as "owning" ACT, so he started attending every ACT workshop and took his data person with him! His teachers began to notice and now see him as "owning" ACT. They are starting to follow his lead and have begun to implement ACT teaching strategies in their CTE courses. Through the process of modeling "ownership of ACT," he has established a collective efficacy among his CTE teachers that they do have the power to influence student performance on the ACT.

By attending and leading each focus-group meeting, you are sending the message that you believe the feedback is important to the vision and mission of the district. You are demonstrating ownership and belief in the Four-Question Model.

## Sample Groups

*Note: Some groups may need to be combined in small districts.*

- Elementary teachers
- Middle school teachers
- High school teachers (core and career and technical education teachers)
- Elementary principals
- Middle school principals
- High school principals
- Assistant principals
- School counselors
- Instructional coaches
- Custodians
- Bus drivers
- Secretaries

- Bookkeepers
- PTA presidents
- Parents of students with disabilities
- Community groups (Chamber of Commerce, Urban League, etc.)
- Ministers or clergy
- Central office staff
- Student council representatives
- Random sample of students across grade levels
- Postsecondary partners
- Business and industry partners

**Sample groups outside of education might include the following:**

- Administrative Assistants
- Account Managers/General Managers
- Auditing/Bookkeeping/Accounting
- Customer Service Representatives
- Customers/Clients
- Salespeople
- Custodial Staff
- Human Resources/Training/Labor Relations
- Production Workers
- Institution and Cafeteria Cooks
- Receptionists
- Maintenance/Repair
- Security Guards
- Landscaping/Grounds-keeping
- Delivery Service Drivers
- Shipping and Receiving

- Packers and Packagers
- Computer Support Specialists/IT

The key is to identify those stakeholder groups that you want to include in crafting a collective vision. Each of the groups above have the power to impact the tipping point of your supervisory success and, ultimately, the success of your organization.

## Analyzing and Sharing the Results

Interpreting the results of the individual surveys and Think-a-Thon debriefing strategy (see the Appendix) is not a quick process. Be prepared to spend time with your leadership team to analyze the qualitative data collected on surveys for each focus-group meeting. Surveys are analyzed using a system of hash marks. Every time a comment is made more than three times, it is written down. If the comment or suggestion is repeated beyond that, a hash mark is placed beside it. Responses with the greatest number of hash marks, along with the impact it is expected to have on teaching and learning, are listed as the top priorities.

The survey results are analyzed for each focus group and collectively as a whole district. District leaders are always amazed when they see feedback from the cafeteria worker being similar to the principals or the bus driver similar to the teachers! Once each focus group's survey results are compiled, all original forms are placed in a book by group with a summary in front of each group. Then, a collective summary of all group responses is placed at the front of the notebook.

Results from the whole-group debriefing strategy are also included in each stakeholder group section. Notebooks can be saved in hard or electronic copies, and every individual who participates in the process should receive a copy of the whole-group summary.

Following the completion of all of the focus-group meetings, feedback should be given to each group. Often common priorities emerge, leading to a connected leadership message to stakeholder groups. If priorities identified are specific to one group, district leaders should provide direct feedback to that group.

There will be a short list of those things that can be addressed immediately and give your district quick wins. Some things may not be able to be accomplished. For example, the highest priority for the third question may be that everyone needs a big raise, but there may not be money to do that. The key is to close the loop back with the groups to let them know why this priority cannot be met now and assure them that it is a priority.

When this process was used in a Kentucky school district, there was strong feedback to the superintendent that there was a need for student interventions that were not punitive. Multiple focus-groups agreed that there were students who just did not fit into the traditional classroom setting. Once the superintendent had evidence that schools had looked at different ways to deliver the curriculum as well as using a variety of instructional strategies to meet diverse student needs, he accepted the group's recommendation to establish an alternative school where these students could be better served.

Once the feedback was shared with the school board, board members agreed that the need existed. They approved a new alternative school—one of the first alternative schools in the state. Those students who had the greatest risk factors for dropping out of school were selected to attend. The alternative setting for these students helped them get back on track to graduate and lowered the dropout rate in the district.

The leadership message you are sending in this process is that you listen and you care about what your constituency has to say. When you make changes based on the feedback, it strengthens your credibility and trust levels. One important note is that you will need to schedule annual stakeholder group surveys, which allows you to continually use this qualitative feedback to inform the agenda year after year. Additionally, you and your leadership team should have processes to listen to stakeholders on a regular basis.

District advisory groups are one way to do this. By hosting annual focus-group meetings, district leaders actually have a re-entry plan every year. This will go a long way in creating buy-in from stakeholders. However, to keep your finger on the district's pulse, establish district advisory committees that meet at least four times a year. You might want to meet with combined groups monthly and scale back if that is too often. The focus of these meetings is to review the district improvement plan and status of the actions taken to address goals in the plan.

Once the focus-group survey data have been summarized, it is time to share results with the school board members. An interesting dynamic about boards of education is the individual members have their own learning styles regarding how they receive and review information. As a leader, one must communicate with the members in ways that meet the needs of the individuals as well as the overall group.

Some board members need to see every detail for every item in writing, whereas others just need a summary in paragraph form. Then there are others who just want a sentence to describe the topic. Knowing how to best communicate with board members is not only needed for this process but also for board meetings and agendas. In the case of the four questions, a whole-group summary must be included along with the actual responses from each individual surveyed. Board members will select what they want to read based on their personal styles.

## TO SUM UP

The Four-Question Model is all about district leaders using a process to develop a continuous-improvement plan with significant stakeholder input, and it gives stakeholders the confidence that what they say really matters. The results help develop an entry plan for a leader to help them get off on the right foot and be successful in the long run.

Your commitment to using this model reflects the fact that you understand school improvement or school turnaround is a journey; you never finish or reach a destination. The next four chapters will build your confidence in using the model. They will also enhance your understanding of how and why this process should be used continuously in your journey to improve your school system.

## REFLECTIVE QUESTIONS AND ACTIVITIES

Suggestions on how to use these reflective questions and activities: Focus Group, Professional Learning Community, District Leadership Team Book Study, or Vertical Leadership Teamwork.

You can answer the questions individually or assign questions and then reconvene as a group to review responses. You might also consider using the Think-a-Thon strategy outlined in the Appendix if you want to come together after reading and answer the questions as a group.

1. List the ways you model at the district level that you are a learning leader.
2. Which step in the process will be the most difficult to implement?
3. What steps can the superintendent delegate and what steps should he or she be directly responsible for conducting?
4. Create a time line for implementing the Four-Question Model in your district or organization.
5. Draft a letter to be sent to focus-group members explaining the process and the importance of their participation.

*Chapter Two*

# What Is Working? Things You Do Not Want to Change

## WHAT'S WORKING AND HOW DO WE KNOW IT'S WORKING?

You are modeling shared leadership by starting with the question, What is working (things you do *not* want to change)? You are also beginning the process on a positive note. In systems where there are serious culture issues, negativity dominates the thought process and people have a hard time even thinking about positives. As you begin to unfold the district's DNA, you will uncover the district culture and climate.

Gruenert and Whitaker (2015) share some differences between culture and climate. They say, "If culture is a school's personality, climate is its attitude" (p. 11). They go on to say it is a lot easier to change an attitude as opposed to a personality. Culture is difficult to change, and they note, "It's always easier to describe what you do (climate) rather than why you do it (culture)" (p. 16). One of the things that makes school improvement and turnaround so difficult is that, "Culture is that black box" (p. 14). That is what makes it so difficult to think outside the box. Climate can shift from happy to sad, but culture is difficult to change.

Your stakeholders will appreciate the opportunity to tell you what they think is working and why. Regardless of how poorly a district is performing, there are always things that are being done successfully. This question forces the negative thinkers into answering from a positive viewpoint. How many schools take the time to stop and think about whether initiatives or practices are making a positive impact on teaching and learning?

If something is working, then the data to support that statement must also be documented. Specific examples of things people did not want to change in one district included: planning time, focus on arts, steps on salary scales based on education, strong staff, and strong discipline policies.

The first question begins the process of determining determine your organization's DNA. Daggett and Gendron (n.d.) discuss DNA in their brief, *What's Your School's DNA? Using Data to Drive Innovation.* They highlight six signs that indicate your strategic plan is falling apart. One of those signs is "Taking the More Is More Approach." They state that although this might be a comprehensive approach, it "can easily overwhelm and does not set schools up for success" (p. 1). They also cite three steps to take when planning for impact: Use data to drive decisions; focus your plan on a shared vision; and cultivate and practice strong leadership (pp. 1–2).

The Four-Question Model works because every district does not have the same DNA. If we could successfully replicate school reform or school turnaround by simply implementing the same initiatives that were successful in one district and copy that exactly in another district, our schools would not be failing. When we overlook different perceptions about a district's DNA, we make a lot of assumptions that lead us to failure. The road to school improvement is littered along the way with failing schools that simply bought into a "promising" program without assessing the district's DNA.

The black box of school reform is filled with the fact that each school has its own DNA, and the district's DNA is made up of all the schools' DNA. If there is a shared vision, you will see common DNA strands. It is up to the leader to help maintain a focus on the vision that helps schools develop these common DNA strands. This is a critical point in understanding how the Four-Question Model can work to build a shared vision that cultivates and practices strong leadership.

## District Leadership Modeling

As you determine your district's and school's DNA, you must start with the question of whether you have the right organizational structure and the right members on your district leadership team. The larger the district, the harder it is to turn around schools. With the right team, your odds for success are higher. Review your vision and mission statements and ask yourself the question, "Are district-level leaders modeling behaviors and beliefs that support those statements?"

Steve Barkley, executive vice president, PLS 3rd Learning, promotes a backward planning model in his book written with Terri Bianco, *Instructional Coaching with the End in Mind* (2011). Backward planning means identifying the student achievement expected and identifying student behavior changes expected. The model backs out through each level of leadership, starting with the teacher and ending at the district leadership level.

When we are not modeling beliefs or behaviors expected of students from the top down, we are less likely to get positive results. This backward planning process will assist in developing a focused vision. For example, if you find a need for differentiation in instruction, you may need to address the belief that all students can learn—just not on the same day or in the same way. You might also find a need to address cooperation—the ability to work with others. Often schools already have the golden keys to change, but the adult behavior has to change first.

There was a school district implementing a school-based reform initiative during the Comprehensive School Reform grant funding back in the early 1990s. During a technical assistance visit, the consultant sat down to interview the superintendent of the district. The superintendent stated, "These kids will never be proficient." The consultant responded, "Not with that attitude." That superintendent is no longer in the district, and the new district vision is: "To empower and inspire each student to achieve excellence." Stop and reflect for a moment on the leader of a district saying that to someone who was coming in to provide reform assistance. Amazing! You know, if the superintendent does not believe in kids, it is unlikely other district and school leaders will believe in them.

Another principal that was working to turn around a school said that at the first faculty meeting he pulled out his driver's license and passed it around. He made every faculty member look at his driver's license. Then he said to the faculty members, "See, I am not Jesus Christ." Wow, you have to really feel for those faculty that had to sit there and pass that driver's license around one by one. The question of, "Why is he doing this?" had to be running through each faculty member's mind. Did he do this because he thought the faculty expected him to perform miracles in student achievement? Was the underlying purpose to send a message that he did not believe the school could raise achievement without a miracle? Did he really believe that IQ is malleable?

If you are looking to establish a culture of mutual respect and trust, you need to remember the human side of change. Most adults in the building are there because they care about kids and want to do the right thing. Treat them with dignity, and know that stakeholders are watching the actions of leaders and often questioning the motive behind the action . . . or inaction.

In one Kentucky district, the superintendent implemented a district motto, "It's About Kids (IAK)." District administrators modeled the practice of making decisions based on what was best for students. The idea was that the district modeling impacts principal and then teacher behavior. Through consistent modeling of this practice, the high school principal began to demonstrate this same decision-making process in the high school, and teachers began demonstrating it in their classrooms. It became so ingrained in some teachers' thought process that it has been a personal practice throughout their career at the classroom, district, state, and national levels.

There are some districts in the country that have this reminder posted in their board rooms: each decision should be based on what is best for students. In a field of education jargon and acronyms, be assured that it is okay to create a new acronym such as "IAK" to send a clear message about what district administrators see as a top priority. Then identify the behaviors staff and stakeholders at all levels should model to reflect the priority.

## What's Your Leadership Style?

By cultivating and practicing strong leadership, the district superintendent or director can establish a trusting culture in the district. Teachers will feel like they could try new teaching strategies, write educational grants, or anything else that would help the students in their classrooms. When teachers believe that district leaders trust them to do what is right for their students and their parents, you begin to build collective efficacy. Dan Ponterfract (2013) identifies this leadership trait in the fourth chapter of his book, *Flat Army: Creating a Connected and Engaged Organization*. He says that to become a connected leader, you have to trust that people want to do what's right and that belief is reciprocal.

For example, when district leaders are making decisions based on what is best for students, you are likely to see school and teacher leaders modeling a reciprocal belief. He goes on to say, "Micro-managing, for example, is merely another name for distrust" (pp. 74–75). If you have worked with both types of leaders, you have your own examples of how their leadership style impacted your work performance. Ponterfract hit the nail on the head when he describes a connected leader. When district leaders communicate their belief in teachers, then district leaders and teachers build a shared trust. This shared trust will make teachers strive to work harder to become a better teacher, and that gives the superintendent an opportunity to recognize those efforts as well.

When a district leader demonstrates trust among teachers, it builds up their confidence. Ponterfract's notes in *Flat Army* that "vulnerability begets trust; trust begets loyalty" (p. 76). On the other hand, working with micromanagers makes teachers feel like they are trapped in a culture Ponterfract uses adjectives to describe such as "distrust or suspicion" (p. 75).

Even when the leader talks about an open-door policy or trusting relationships, their actions speak louder than words. Staff know when they truly have "access" to school or district leaders. When leaders value the organizational hierarchy or the organizational chart more than the mission, they are not connected leaders.

Liz Wiseman has a similar perspective on leadership styles. She writes about two different leadership styles in her book, *Multipliers* (2010). She refers to the two leadership styles as multipliers and diminishers. Wiseman analyzed data from more than 150 leaders and found that people who work for multipliers put forth two times more effort than when they worked for a diminisher. A diminisher got less than half of people's intelligence and capability—about 48 percent (p. 11). There is a human side to change that great leaders do not overlook. Wiseman talks about how multipliers recognize the genius in their team members, and they build on these strengths.

In one Kentucky teacher's first position, her department chair was a diminisher. The teacher received a $1,000 grant to do a community-based project. Her department chair called her a "Glory Seeker," but she was never quite sure how a $1,000 grant made her a "Glory Seeker." For her, it was more about establishing community partnerships and planning engaging lessons. Isn't it amazing how we as students never forget the power of our teachers' words? In the same vein, we as adults are also impacted by the words of other adults—both the multipliers and the diminishers.

You will know a diminisher when you meet this style of manager. They are the person who is hiring highly qualified people. Then the manager makes all the decisions and does not get their input. As opposed to a multiplier, the diminisher does not encourage the team members to pursue advancement opportunities. If questions are asked in meetings, answers are not listened to because the diminisher always wants to be the smartest person in the room.

It does not take a new teacher long to determine what leadership style they are dealing with in a principal or superintendent. The multiplier is asking questions and getting input, so their decisions are implemented more quickly. A diminisher, as the smartest person in the room, has to fire off quick decisions without garnering input. People are left asking, "Why are we doing this?" So, decisions are implemented more slowly and less effectively. Trust me, it does not take a new teacher very long to sum up the school and district leadership culture.

In today's age of "priority, focus, and target" schools, we often see new offices of innovation or school turnaround being established. Often, district leaders bring in a new "superstar" to lead this work. Unfortunately, these leaders gather a group of district staff and chart a plan based on turnaround theory; when they could learn so much more by asking stakeholders in these failing schools four simple questions. However, not all diminishers set out to become a diminisher; Wiseman calls them "accidental diminishers" (p. 29).

The mere practice of implementing this Four-Question Model can help prevent organizational leaders from becoming "accidental diminishers." You do not have to prove that you are the smartest person in the room by having all the answers. Sometimes the most powerful person in the room is the person demonstrating the power of silence (silent power) and engaged listening. As you lead the Focus Group meetings, remember to model this silent power. If it is difficult for you to do so, you may be on the path of the "accidental diminisher."

Adults in the workplace do not typically make mistakes purposely. For the most part, they want to do the right thing, especially teachers. When mistakes happen, it may be because the adults have not been trained properly or do not know where to go to ask for help. It could just be that they just don't know what they don't know. If things "bubble up" to you as a superintendent, you have two options. You can launch an investigation, or you can go to the district or school leader and have an open, honest conversation and let them know you believe they want to do the right thing.

Taking the time to sit down and converse with them will demonstrate that you care about them as a person and care less about gossip. Based on Wiseman's research on multipliers, you will end up getting more productivity from them in the long run. If you really believe that "it's about kids," then you take the time to remind everyone that the focus is on student learning. Sometimes we all need a reminder of how our actions impact this critical goal.

Would things look differently in our school turnaround or school improvement work if leaders began to restrain themselves more and listening to others? What if they took the time to become skilled in the art of asking the right questions? This Four-Question Model can help district leaders identify barriers, challenges, and solutions in the system and bring a sense of inquiry into a district-wide decision-making process.

## TO SUM UP

You are taking the time to recognize the hard work and effort stakeholders are putting forth to fully implement initiatives that have a positive impact on teaching and learning when you start with the question, What is working (things you do *not* want to change)?. A side benefit of asking this question is that you are also getting an unspoken commitment from stakeholders that they will continue their efforts to make these initiatives successful.

As you reflect on the qualitative data results from using this four-step model, think about how you demonstrate "ownership" of these initiatives at the district level. Are you using a backward modeling approach? Ultimately, it is a moral issue; educators and stakeholders all want the best for students in the system. Your role as leader in asking this question is to help stakeholders identify what is working and recognize their efforts in making it work. Be a "multiplier" and remember that you do not always have to be the smartest person in the room.

## REFLECTIVE QUESTIONS AND ACTIVITIES

Suggestions on how to use these reflective questions and activities: Focus Group, Professional Learning Community, District Leadership Team Book Study, or Vertical Leadership Teamwork.

You can answer the questions individually or assign questions and then reconvene as a group to review responses. You might also consider using the Think-a-Thon strategy outlined in the Appendix if you want to come together after reading and answer the questions as a group.

1. How will this process create a connected and engaged organization?
2. What are some district initiatives you think are working (things you do *not* want to change)?
3. What are the top three initiatives you think others see your leadership team as "owning"?
4. Identify two student behaviors and backward-map those behaviors from teacher, principal, to district leader behaviors you are already modeling or want to model.
5. Consider a district leadership team book study on Liz Wiseman's book, *Multipliers*, or Dan Ponterfract's book, *Flat Army*.

*Chapter Three*

# What Needs to Be Changed to Make This a Better Place for Kids?

## CHRISTMAS TREES AND KITCHEN SINKS

Picture a plate where you are piling on more and more food. Eventually, you will run out of room. You cannot put more on the plates of educators if you do not make room first. Most of the resistance experienced in education turnaround work has been because teachers have too much on their plates. Across the country, teachers are telling us they do not have enough time to do all that is expected of them. Districts and schools that keep adding new initiatives and programs are Christmas-tree or kitchen-sink school systems that just keep dumping more and more on educators.

There are large urban school districts that have received millions in school-improvement funding. Money is certainly beneficial to a low-performing school, but often schools end up adding programs to the school as opposed to a well-thought district- or school-improvement plan. Some schools have so many competing initiatives, that they have no choice but to rebrand the school. Other districts simply choose to restart a failing school, and most often the school reopens to serve the same student population—but under new district leadership with a sense of urgency to improve the status quo.

Sometimes it gets to the point where old initiatives are reintroduced, and faculty are again seen wearing their T-shirts, "Been there, done that." That is not to say that there may indeed be new circumstances that merit an initiative being reintroduced, but it is a reminder of what kind of resistance these initiatives face when you have veteran faculty who were on staff the last time the initiative was unsuccessful. New initiatives, programs, and processes bring about new requirements with greater time demands. Something has to give.

Richard Huseman and Merwyn Hayes wrote *The Secret of the Hidden Paycheck* (2001). Most teachers can really relate to the idea of the hidden paycheck because they are not in the field of education so that they can make a lot of money. If you want to establish trust with educators, you have to make deposits of trust in a bank account. When you realize it is not about the money, and you start giving teachers more time to collaborate, for example, you will get more from them in terms of performance. The bottom line in educational improvement is when you start meeting people's needs, they will work harder to meet educational goals. If you are not asking them the right questions, you will never know what needs truly exist.

The only thing we cannot add along with new initiatives is time in the workweek to implement them—unless we stop spending time on old initiatives that are not working. It is time to address the elephant in the room. Stop doing things just because it is the way they have always been done. Do instead the things that make a difference.

## Student Voice

Your student focus group will really enjoy answering the question, "What is not working?" because it is about them! Kallick and Zmuda (2017) talk about how we can empower students. They note that "we must include opportunities for all students to build social capital and develop a voice for interaction with people in power positions. They (students) must learn how to create and use professional networks and develop and promote their innovative ideas" (p. 1). What a perfect way to promote student empowerment—having a student focus group with district leaders!

One high school principal planned and implemented a student advocacy program. The principal had an advocacy team that designed and developed a curriculum for advocacy meetings based on grade level. Once teachers were trained, the advocacy program was successfully implemented, and every student in the school had an opportunity to develop a relationship with one adult role model. As Josh Shipp says, "Every kid is one caring adult away from being a success story."

After the school had implemented the advocacy program, two important events happened in this school. The first one involved an outside review team that visited the school and interviewed stakeholders, including students. They asked a group of seniors, "We noticed the school has implemented a lot of changes over the past two years, such as the advocacy program. How do you feel about that?" One student responded, "They are only doing it because they care about us." The second event was when two freshmen girls went to their advocacy teacher and told him that they were concerned about a fellow freshman who was carrying around a large gym bag. The teacher went to school leaders, and they removed the freshman from the auditorium where 450 fellow freshmen were seated. School leaders discovered several weapons and a pipe bomb inside the gym bag. Thanks to the leaders and faculty in this school who were willing to be the caring adult for each child in the school, a serious situation was diverted.

It is also worthy to note that these teachers looped with their advocacy group for all four years of high school. The first graduating class stood up row by row to receive their high school diploma. As they exited the row, heading to the stage, they went over and hugged their teacher advocate. A true testament that the school had made it a better place for kids!

At the district level, one superintendent established, "Stu's Crew," with whom he had a monthly lunch to get their input on their educational experience. Students were randomly selected and represented a diverse cross-section of the schools. Not only did the superintendent receive great feedback, but the process also became a communication loop for principals. School leaders awaited the students return, so they could be sure to make needed adjustments on issues students had just shared with the superintendent.

## Weeding the Garden

Each of the focus groups will bring ideas to the table about what needs to be taken off their plates. Doug Reeves refers to the process of removing initiatives and policies from educators' plates as weeding your garden in his book, *Leading Change in Your School: How to Conquer Myths, Build Commitment, and Get Results* (2009). Reeves calls the process a "garden party" (p. 15). In his 2006a Educational Leadership article, "Leading to Change/Pull the Weeds Before You Plant the Flowers," Reeves lays out a strategy to weed the garden.

Reeves has educators list every initiative started in the last five years. Then he has them list every initiative that has been discontinued. He says the first list is always significantly longer (pp. 89–90). Just because a process, program, or initiative has been in place for years does not mean it is having a positive impact on student learning. Take stock of what is taking time away from improving instruction across the district, schools, and classrooms.

It is important for leaders and teachers to think about to what extent all of their initiatives are theoretically consistent. Are there initiatives in place that conflict each other? Step out of the box; discontinue a process, program, or initiative; give your school leaders and teachers what they want most: more time.

In *First Break all the Rules: What the World's Greatest Managers Do Differently*, Marcus Buckingham and Curt Coffman (2008) look at what separates great managers from the rest. The two Gallup analysts drew their insights from twenty-five years of Gallup studies of eighty thousand managers across four hundred companies. What they found is that the greatest managers had different backgrounds and styles. Yet, even with all of their differences, great managers shared one common trait: "They don't hesitate to break virtually every rule held sacred by conventional wisdom" (p. 11). They were not afraid to weed the garden.

## Creating Buy-in on the Front End

Using the Four-Question Model is a much more cost-effective way to garner stakeholder input than hiring an outside consulting firm. Asking stakeholders what is working provides some qualitative feedback in the change process and creates buy-in. Leadership author, John Maxwell, says, "People buy into the leader before they buy into the vision" (2013). Therefore, when you personally conduct these sessions, the buy-in process begins. As people buy into the leader, the leader is building credibility and trust.

Any district administrator who takes on a job with his or her own agenda will miss an opportunity for valuable stakeholder input. Many educators could tell you stories about how their districts bring in outside consulting firms (spending millions of dollars) to interview stakeholders and then they give the superintendent a written report. Unfortunately, many times the report is used as leverage to further the superintendent's agenda or nothing more is done with the report beyond reading it.

One urban district signed a contract to pay $6.3 million to a foreign company only to have the company tell the district that there was too much central office bureaucracy. The contract was canceled two years in, and the report had little impact in improving teaching and learning across the district. It is likely that a group of stakeholders in that district could have come up with the same feedback for a lot less money.

Another superintendent received invaluable input on how he could make the district and schools a better place for kids. An overwhelming response was to create an environment without interruptions and distractions. Examples included intercom interruptions, disruptive students, and unplanned schedule changes. There was the need to lessen the load by having concrete policies in place for student discipline and communications. This feedback paved the way for the superintendent to put the focus back on teaching and learning—a focus that supported the district's vision and mission.

Another superintendent empowered high school principals to remove low-level tracks and require all students to complete college-prep level courses. This was a major shift that helped the district move from an ability model to an effort model. There was some resistance from faculty who did not believe "those kids" could do college-prep level work. The district and schools reevaluated their belief system.

A couple of years after the change was implemented, and students were no longer tracked, the high school went on to win three National Blue Ribbon awards and was recognized as a New American High School. Later, the high school Special Education coordinator was asked, "What do you think about us removing the low-level tracks?" The Special Education coordinator responded, "It think it is great. It bumped up the expectations for all of the students in this school, including special education students."

## College and Career Readiness

One thing that needs to change to make schools a better place for kids is to better understand what college and career readiness is all about. We hear a lot about college and career readiness, but community and education stakeholders lack a clear vision of what it would look like in their school district or schools. You cannot take the college-going culture in this country and change it quickly.

If you can help a student leaving high school meet college- and career-readiness standards, they are more likely to be successful in whatever path they choose. When students leave high school with an industry-recognized credential in a high-demand, high-wage, and high-skilled field, they are more employable for a middle- or high-income job. If the student chooses to go back to school later, they can. Often employers have tuition-reimbursement programs, so students are less likely to leave with a huge college debt.

Being college and career ready does not mean choosing a career or college after high school. It means that these paths are intertwined because the majority of jobs today do not require a four-year degree. However, they do require some education beyond high school, such as an industry-recognized credential or apprenticeship.

Nursing is a great example in the health field. A certified nurse assistant (CNA) can land a job right out of high school, earning significantly more than a graduate with just a high school diploma. After working as a CNA, that student might decide to go back and become a licensed practical nurse (LPN) or registered nurse (RN). If they stay on the postsecondary pathway, they could eventually become a doctor.

College and career readiness means offering students career pathways that align to labor market data as well as postsecondary options. The Four-Question Model is a great way to start the conversation in a district to make the cultural shift from, "everyone's going to college" to "everyone is going to be college and career ready."

The question, "What needs to be changed to make this a better place for kids?" must address college and career readiness. Debriefing this question with your district and school leadership stakeholders will allow you to establish goals and action steps toward a common understanding and definition of college and career readiness.

One superintendent asked this question and received feedback from multiple stakeholder focus groups on the need for more technology integration. It was easy to see how technology was impacting jobs across the United States—everything from small tech companies to manufacturing. Knowing that practically every job of the future would be touched by technology, the district went on to establish one of the state's first one-to-one laptop initiatives for high school students. Teacher feedback led to a process that included a pilot year and a newly appointed staff developer position that worked with pilot teachers on integrating technology across the curriculum. Principals and teachers also said they wanted to implement the one-to-one laptop initiative incrementally, so the district created a roll-out plan over the next four years. This is another example of how the Four-Question Model can position a school district to be on the cutting edge.

## TO SUM UP

Why are educators more likely to start initiatives than to discontinue old initiatives? Most likely, they are not basing decisions on data, or they are not asking for input from those who are directly impacted by initiatives. We need to spend more time looking at what is not working and on changes that could have a significant impact on student achievement. We need to ask the question: "What needs to be changed to make this a better place for kids?" Weeding the garden will help the seeds of knowledge grow.

# REFLECTIVE QUESTIONS AND ACTIVITIES

Suggestions on how to use these reflective questions and activities: Focus Group, Professional Learning Community, District Leadership Team Book Study, or Vertical Leadership Teamwork.

You can answer the questions individually or assign questions and then reconvene as a group to review responses. You might also consider using the Think-a-Thon strategy outlined in the Appendix if you want to come together after reading and answer the questions as a group.

1. What are the top three initiatives in your district you feel are being fully implemented?
2. Are there any concerns your leadership team has about weeding the garden?
3. What things do leadership team members agree can stop being implemented at the district level? Why?
4. What things do you predict will be the top five things school principals will list for this question?
5. Make a list of all the initiatives your district or organization has started in the past five years. Make a list of all the initiatives that have been discontinued. Which list in longer?

*Chapter Four*

# What Needs to Be Changed to Make This a Better Place for Adults?

## HUMAN SIDE OF CHANGE

The question, "What needs to be changed to make this a better place for adults?" sends a clear message that you understand there is a human side to change. Stephen Covey said, "There are three constants in life . . . change, choice and principles." In business and education, we are constantly seeking ways to improve. However, in order to improve, we will have to experience change. This question allows you, as the leader, to demonstrate lifelong learning. There may be some basic human needs that you have not discovered as the leader that can help your faculty truly implement professional learning communities, fully implement new teaching strategies, or embrace lifelong learning themselves. If principals or teachers have a basic need in the workplace that is not being met, it is unlikely that their conversations will focus on improving teaching and learning. By asking this question, you are establishing a collaborative conversation with adults who hold the key to school improvement. Ultimately, you will lead these changes, and relationship building will increase your likelihood of success in doing so.

It is important to realize that working with teachers' associations or unions is critical as is being a teacher advocate and not an opponent. In one district, the superintendent took focus-group feedback to the board, and together they set a goal to have the highest teacher salaries in the state.

In *Social Network Theory and Educational Change*, Daly (2010) says that if you are going to try to understand the organization's performance, you have to examine the attributes of the individual stakeholders as well as the relationships that present barriers or opportunities for advancement (pp. 18–19). In examining leadership and social networks, Daly notes the importance of developing a culture of trust and risk-taking for innovative change to occur. He states, "The district must find ways to provide greater opportunities for interaction of individuals in similar (e.g., principals) or different (e.g., principal-central office) positions" (p. 194).

Understanding social networks and establishing stakeholder focus-group meetings will move you further on the connected leader continuum. Fullan also talks about the importance of viewing knowledge as a social phenomenon in *Leading in a Culture of Change* (2001). He states, "if you remember one thing about information, it is that it only becomes valuable in a social context" (p. 78).

By conducting these focus groups and using the Four-Question Model, leaders can build those social networks and take information to the knowledge-creation and -sharing levels. Do not get caught up in one of life's greatest ironies that Fullan describes, "schools are in the business of teaching and learning, yet they are terrible at learning from each other" (p. 90).

## Top-Down and Grassroots Effort

The focus-group meetings and Four-Question Model allow a space for top-down and grassroots practitioners to individually reflect and dialogue as a group—sharing their perspectives. Evans (1996) notes, "just because something seems self-evident and useful to an observer doesn't make its adoption easy for a practitioner" (p. 227). By asking what you can do to make this a better place for adults, you can begin to identify initiatives that never made it past the initial implementation phase.

One large urban school system worked to develop and implement an advisory program. A group of teachers formed a focus team and worked all spring and summer to develop the curriculum and training materials. On the first day of training, not one administrator was present in the room. When the principal was asked why he was not participating in the professional development, he said that he was "ordering desks." Was it more important for that leader to order desks or participate in a program that would provide every child with one adult role model?

The actions of district and school leaders greatly impact the success of new initiatives. In this case, the program failed during the initial-implementation phase. The teachers never really believed they had the principal's support. The next year, they were wearing the T-shirt, "Been there, done that."

You will also encounter staff and faculty that are reluctant to implement new processes or programs. As he describes authentic leaders, Evans talks about understanding reluctant faculty. He states that "many improvement schemes, rooted in diagnosis of current illnesses and the prescription of ideal cures, cures that emphasize positions, policies, and procedures rather than people" (1996, p. 91). Do not be the type of leader that underestimates the power of relationships. Every school system has room to make changes to make it a better place for adults to lead and learn.

## Symbolism

Symbolism is critical to school culture. In one school district, the superintendent shut down access to Google because the new finance software needed more bandwidth. No one communicated this to the district instructional technology coordinators, so they were getting calls from teachers who had "Google Classrooms." It became a fiasco that led to a running joke, "We changed the sign out front to the 'Board of Finance'." Even though this never happened, staff still had the visual in their minds and knew the decision had negatively impacted teaching and learning.

One district superintendent said that when he arrived at central office, there was a feeling that the schools existed to serve the district office rather than vice versa. The solution was to put up a new sign in front of the building indicating what the district mission is: "IAK—It's About Kids." The superintendent renamed the building "It's About Kids Support Services," and had the career and technical students in the brick masonry program build it. The superintendent paid for all the material so nobody could complain that there was a waste of district money.

Constituents also are highly aware of symbolism. District administrators often spend time traveling to and from and visiting schools, but they do not often notice important symbols that constituents will notice as they travel by schools. For example, if the clock on top of the district central office building is broken, it sends out a message that the district is broken. One superintendent had a clock on top of one district building that never had the right time. It could be seen by thousands of people traveling to work every day, and it sent out a message that the district could not fix a simple problem. The superintendent had the clock repaired and made sure it had the correct time at all times!

Another change the superintendent made to make the district a better place for adults and improve district culture was the implementation of a 24-hour return communication policy. All communication was required to be answered within 24 hours. This created somewhat of a problem for the superintendent as district leader because he was receiving 800 e-mails, letters, and calls in his first months at the district. He was staying up until 5:00 a.m. and starting his new day at 7:00 a.m.

The key was that as school superintendent, he could not ask others to follow a policy if he violated it. According to the superintendent, that policy was a game changer. This is a perfect example of Steve Barkley's backward planning model outlined in chapter 2.

## Recognizing the "Super Stars"

Another game changer is finding a way to recognize high-performing staff. Buckingham and Coffman say that you need to invest time in your best staff. When they interviewed great managers, they said that, "investing in their best was, first, the fairest thing to do; second, the best way to learn; and, third, the only way to stay focused on excellence" (2008, p. 155).

Superintendents can learn a lot from this Gallup research. Instead of trying to win over negative people or naysayers, spend your time highlighting principals and teachers who are going above and beyond.

In one district's turnaround department, the turnaround schools actually gave out an "Above and Beyond" trophy at the start of faculty meetings each month to recognize the Super Stars. As Evans notes that "the single best low-cost, high-leverage way to improve performance, morale, and the climate for change is to dramatically increase the levels of meaningful recognition for—and among—educators. As I use it here, recognition refers to praise or positive feedback, but also to validation, to acknowledging and affirming a truth about a person or a situation" (1996, p. 254).

Whatever process you choose to recognize those who do an outstanding job, just make sure that it is a continuous process so that everyone gets an opportunity to be recognized at some point because you believe in them and know that everyone wants to do the right thing for students in their heart. And tread carefully because the easiest things to see are important but so are the heroic acts that are less visible.

One teacher spoke about how her principal recognized her teacher-leadership skills and asked her to coordinate several reform initiatives that led to the high school being recognized as a "New American High School." Stepping into that leadership role helped shape her future in education. In that same district, her superintendent recognized her leadership skills and asked her to oversee a local community and technical college (CTE) campus that served nine high schools. Establishing a culture of collegiality and trust moves everyone in the upward direction, including students.

That superintendent was modeling at the district level and paying attention to who was modeling at the school level. Todd Whitaker (2012) calls this recognizing the Super Stars; he says to put your time and effort in those who are willing to be the movers and the shakers. Listen to the naysayers and respect them, but invest your time in those who can model and demonstrate to those around them. As Fullan (2001) says, "Ultimately, your leadership in a culture of change will be judged as effective or ineffective not by who you are as a leader but by what leadership you produce in others" (p. 137).

## Dealing with Naysayers

District leaders need to not only understand how to recognize the Super Stars, but they also need to understand how to deal with the naysayers. Gruenert and Whitaker (2015) said this about naysayers in *School Culture Rewired*, "Negative teachers want to avoid joining the battle for a better school while taking potshots at the risk-takers blazing new trails. Having mistaken cynicism for wisdom, these negative teachers might very well believe that they are fighting the good fight and protecting the school. They need to be perceived as the weakest members of the new culture" (p. 162). Naysayers may be the weakest members, but Fullan notes, "If you include and value naysayers, noise in the early stages will yield later, greater implementation" (2001, p. 75).

## The Abilene Paradox

To honor both of these statements regarding Super Stars and Naysayers, the Abilene Paradox may be helpful. The Abilene Paradox was coined by Jerry B. Harvey, Professor Emeritus of

Management at the George Washington University and author of *The Abilene Paradox and Other Meditations on Management*. The paradox is explained using a parable of a family who ends up making an uncomfortable trip that none of them wanted to make in the first place.

> On a hot afternoon visiting in Coleman, Texas, the family is comfortably playing dominoes on a porch, until the father-in-law suggests that they take a trip to Abilene [53 miles north] for dinner. The wife says, "Sounds like a great idea." The husband, despite having reservations because the drive is long and hot, thinks that his preferences must be out-of-step with the group and says, "Sounds good to me. I just hope your mother wants to go." The mother-in-law then says, "Of course I want to go. I haven't been to Abilene in a long time."
>
> The drive is hot, dusty, and long. When they arrive at the cafeteria, the food is as bad as the drive. They arrive back home four hours later, exhausted.
>
> One of them dishonestly says, "It was a great trip, wasn't it?" The mother-in-law says that, actually, she would rather have stayed home, but went along since the other three were so enthusiastic. The husband says, "I wasn't delighted to be doing what we were doing. I only went to satisfy the rest of you." The wife says, "I just went along to keep you happy. I would have had to be crazy to want to go out in the heat like that." The father-in-law then says that he only suggested it because he thought the others might be bored.
>
> The group sits back, perplexed that they together decided to take a trip which none of them wanted. They each would have preferred to sit comfortably, but did not admit to it when they still had time to enjoy the afternoon.

The Four-Question Model provides individual group members an opportunity to voice their opinion and not feel that they must go along with the group. Sometimes it is better to "rock the boat" than to take a trip to Abilene on a hot Texas day.

## TO SUM UP

In school turnaround work, understanding the human side of change is critical to get the adults in the building to change their behavior. Believe they want to do the right thing, and you may turn your naysayer into your biggest cheerleader. Finding ways to recognize those who are working smart and hard is one way to impact the culture in a district and school. Whether you are putting in a new faculty workroom or providing faculty daycare, there is always something your district can do to make it a better place for the adults in the system.

## REFLECTIVE QUESTIONS AND ACTIVITIES

Suggestions on how to use these reflective questions and activities: Focus Group, Professional Learning Community, District Leadership Team Book Study, or Vertical Leadership Teamwork.

You can answer the questions individually or assign questions and then reconvene as a group to review responses. You might also consider using the Think-a-Thon strategy outlined in the Appendix if you want to come together after reading and answer the questions as a group.

1. How would you rate the level of trust between central office and schools on a scale of 1 (lowest) to 10 (highest)?
2. In what ways can the Four-Question Model improve trust among stakeholders?
3. Does your district office have Super Stars? Naysayers? How do you know?
4. How do you recognize Super Stars at the school level?
5. Create a symbolism T-chart. On one side list those that positively reflect the district office, and on the other side, list those that send a negative message about the district office.

*Chapter Five*

# What Can I Do, as Your Leader, to Do a Better Job?

## A LEARNING LEADER IS VULNERABLE

Demonstrate your vulnerability as a leader by asking the final question, "What can I do, as your leader, to do a better job?" You cannot expect other adults in the system to change if you are not modeling change at the district level. As you model vulnerability, you are laying the foundation blocks of trust as you model your willingness to accept feedback and implement leadership change.

Warren Berger interviewed Paul Bennett, longtime creative director at the innovation firm IDEO, for his book, *A More Beautiful Question* (2014). Bennett talked about establishing a culture that engenders trust and said that "part of questioning is about exposing vulnerability—and being okay with vulnerability as a cultural currency" (p. 78). One teacher reflected back to her first year of college, and one of her instructors was talking to her about becoming an educator. The instructor said "it doesn't matter if you have the right answer—what matters is if you know where to find the answer, and sometimes there is more than one answer." In other words, you don't have to be the smartest person in the room.

That teacher has worked in districts where the leader felt like they had to demonstrate that they had all the right answers. When leaders accept the fact that they do not have to prove that they have all the right answers, they will be ready to ask the right questions. When we as adults model the right questioning techniques, we set the stage for other district and school leaders to follow our example.

One strategy you can use when you visit classrooms is to jot down question stems used by both teachers and students. It does not take long to evaluate the level of questioning being asked by teachers and students. In some schools, teachers are asking the majority of questions. One teacher decided to use Bloom's Taxonomy to teach his students how to ask high-level questions. Now that is a best practice in education! If you, as the superintendent, want your principals, teachers, and students asking high-level questions, remember you are their best role model.

Using the Four-Question Model positions you as the district leader in a vulnerable role that others will observe during this innovative inquiry process. Berger (2014) also interviewed Jim Hackett about becoming the new CEO of Steelcase. Hackett struggled, initially, with what this role should look like. Over time, he found that his role as a leader was to "look at the chaos and provide a point of view about what needs to be done." Hackett maintains that projecting a clear and distinctive view others can follow is key to effective leadership, "but that clear vision is arrived at, and constantly modified and sharpened, through deep reflection and questioning" (p. 161).

Kegan and Lahey (2001) note that "it is very hard to lead on behalf of other people's changes in their underlying ways of making meaning without considering the possibility that we ourselves must also change" (p. 3). When superintendents ask this question in focus-group meetings, they show vulnerability to their stakeholders. Even the best teachers make themselves vulnerable every day. Students see this vulnerability, and they realize learning is lifelong. A by-product of this process is that change is an expectation and the norm.

As normal procedure in his district, one superintendent sat down with a newly appointed elementary school principal, Meribeth. She reflected on her conversation with the superintendent and his advice on a process that would help establish a collaborative and transparent culture from day one. Meribeth used the Four-Question Model to find out what staff members valued most. By using the right questions, she was able to discern what faculty felt was working and what needed to improve. Meribeth learned that teachers wanted more time to collaborate, and they wanted meeting times to be purposeful. The teachers also expressed a desire to see their work valued. She learned that valuing their work, time, and commitment set forth a model for how she expected them to respond to students. It was a critically defined domino effect. As a new leader, she discovered that the school needed a process to recognize both students and staff for jobs well done!

Meribeth felt it was essential to learn faculty expectations of her as their new principal. Many had never been asked such a question before, and some were not sure how to respond. It was an eye-opening and rewarding experience for all because it gave autonomy to the staff and new-found voice. She saved the question, "What can I do as your leader to do a better job?" as a mid-year check. She surveyed each staff member before winter break to determine how well they thought she was meeting their expectations. Their feedback was important to her in determining next steps as she modified the plan for support moving forward. The use of the Four-Question Model began a professional conversation with her staff that continued and improved during Meribeth's tenure at the school.

By asking this question, "What can I do as your leader to do a better job?", you are modeling the Learning Leadership dimensions outlined in *The Learning Leader: How to Focus School Improvement for Better Results* (2006b). In it, Reeves describes the "visionary leader" and how leaders can use vision to build trust and notes that "commitment depends upon knowing one's personal role in the vision and seeing a clear path to how to get there" (p. 38). An earlier example of this was the It's About Kids (IAK) initiative. The superintendent created a collective vision that built trust around a focus on kids. Relational leadership is another leadership dimension Reeves discusses.

If you are serious about improving as a district superintendent, you will need the skills of a "relational leader." According to Reeves, "relational leaders listen without interrupting or prejudging, respecting confidentiality, giving genuine empathy through deliberate inquiry" (p. 40). The Four-Question Model paves the way for relational leadership. Providing time for stakeholders to answer important questions allows the superintendent to model relational leadership.

Reeves (2006b) also mentions the leader as an architect. As an architectural leader, you practice distributed leadership because you realize that one person cannot possess all of the skills necessary for effective organizational leadership. So, you "hire and retain complementary leaders—people with different skill sets, intelligences, and behavioral characteristics" (p. 29). Once you have a compelling agenda in place, putting the right people in "the right seats on the bus" is critical. The Four-Question Model will help you hone these leadership dimensions and continually improve as a district leader.

## Visioning and Establishing Purpose

As district leader, you are responsible for crafting a compelling mission and vision—the improvement map that will give people directions to a common goal. "Often cited as helping set directions are such specific practices as identifying and articulating a vision, fostering the acceptance of group goals and creating high performance expectations. Visioning and establishing purpose are also enhanced by monitoring organizational performance and promoting effective communication and collaboration" (Leithwood et al., 2004, p. 24).

You will find out quickly who the "internal influencers" are in the district. Make a point to create an "opinion-influencers" mailing list, and use this list to keep internal influencers aware of progress or barriers that the district faces in accomplishing the annual improvement plan.

One district brought in an outside group to conduct a technical assistance review of a failing high school. One of the members of the group was also the city's director of economic development, and he was putting together a campaign committee to run for mayor. This person kept bringing up the fact that the school's new superintendent bought a home out in the county—out of city limits. Being aware of opinion-influencers helped this superintendent understand that this perception was a reality that she had to deal with, and she made sure to include him in her weekly newsletters that highlighted best practices across the district. It pays to know your internal influencers as well as your opinion-influencers and keep them informed regarding district progress and next steps—especially if you are a new superintendent!

Whether you are assuming your first superintendent job or you are assuming a superintendent position in a new district, the Four-Question Model is a strong strategy that can create stakeholder buy-in to the district mission and vision. Communication skills are critical in this process. It is important that leaders listen closely to focus-group feedback both in the initial meetings and then, again, annually. It will flag areas that need improvement and will strengthen the leadership team.

The goal is to "listen to the whispers before they become screams." As Willink and Babin (2015) note, "Remember, it's not about you. . . . It's about the mission and how best to accomplish it. With that attitude exemplified in you and your key leaders, your team will dominate" (p. 105).

## A Clear Communication Plan

Having a clear communication plan to share the survey and focus-group results is imperative. Evans (1996) states that "change begins not just with a goal but with a leader who communicates it, enlisting the organization's members in the pursuit of a compelling agenda" (p. 201). When you complete this Four-Question Model, stakeholders will feel valued, and you will create buy-in for the improvement plan if you have a clear communication plan.

Reeves (2006b) refers to this fourth leadership dimension as communicative leadership, stating that "leaders underestimate the power of personalized communication and overestimate the effectiveness of hierarchical communication" (p. 58). Make sure your communication plan includes personalized communication strategies to various stakeholder participants. Once you have identified the school community's needs, then you can match the communication plan to those stakeholders.

## Celebrate Victories

Maxwell (2013) talks about celebrating victories in his online blog. "A big vision is filled with many small goals. Celebrating victories in those areas helps team members track their progress and find the motivation to continue on the journey." Celebrating small steps toward your goals can have a powerfully positive impact on the district culture.

Amabile and Kramer's article, "The Power of Small Wins" (2011), addresses the idea of celebrating victories. The authors provide the example of James Watson and Francis Crick as they attempted to build the first scientific DNA model. Their first few attempts failed, but when they had a model their colleagues could not find fault with, Watson wrote in his memoir that his morale skyrocketed.

Amabile and Kramer analyzed diaries of other knowledge workers and discovered the "Progress Principle: Of all the things that can boost emotions, motivation, and perceptions during a workday, the single most important is making progress in meaningful work. And the more frequently people experience that sense of progress, the more likely they are to be creatively productive in the long run." To improve or turn around a district, you will need innovative workers. Based on the Progress Principle, your plan will need to include what and how you will celebrate small steps toward reaching your goals.

Quinn, Heynoski, Thomas, and Spreitzer (2014) studied the most highly effective teachers in several states over a period of years. They found that highly effective teachers exhibit practices reflecting a stable environment and continuous improvement. As they describe "collective learning," teachers talk about shifting from a classroom environment where they feared the loss of control to an environment where they relaxed control and trusted their students to engage at a high level.

One teacher spoke about focusing on learning and paying attention to what her students were teaching her: "When the energy is high . . . I can look out and see it. . . . it's literally something. I don't know how to describe it. I can feel there is energy in the room. Everyone's brain-waves are making connections or making motion or something like that" (Quinn et al., 2014, p. 83). Some call this the productive struggle, but Quinn and colleagues might call this the Progress Principle!

If as the district leader, you fear the loss of control, you cannot model continuous improvement, innovation, and creativity. When you are not modeling these things, you are more likely to see teacher-centered classrooms in your schools.

## Collective Capacity

This Four-Question Model can serve any superintendent well. It charts a pathway for stakeholder input and a process for continuous school improvement. Imagine the leadership pipeline we could develop if we modeled this process at the district, school, and classroom levels. As Fullan notes that "in a culture of complexity, the chief role of leadership is to mobilize the collective capacity to challenge difficult circumstances" (2001, p. 136).

To accomplish this collective capacity, you must ask the right questions to determine your district's DNA and craft a continuous-improvement plan with valuable stakeholder input. If you can remove "self" from the equation, you will be better able to focus on the mission—and it just might be the greatest influencer on your leadership style.

After one superintendent administered the Four-Question Model, he was able to take the input received and develop a 13-Year Graduation Plan for incoming kindergarten students that would impact their entire educational experience in the school system. The brain development plan, which landed the district on NBC's *TODAY*, provided foreign language instruction, piano lessons, health and fitness experiences, chess and higher-order thinking skills, exposure to the arts, and behavioral alternatives. For each class entering kindergarten, the district developed a deep community partnership that provided financial support for their sponsoring class.

The components of the graduation plan came out of input from the Four-Question Model. Teams were created to develop each of the components. Because the input came from a wide range of stakeholders, there was huge buy-in from the teachers, parents, administrators, support staff, and the overall community. This example shows how the Four-Question Model can provide a vehicle for those big, bold initiatives that require significant support and buy-in to be successful and sustainable.

Do not be the "Seagull Manager" that Blanchard, Zigarmi, and Zigarmi describe in *Leadership and the One Minute Man-*

*ager* (2000). "Seagull managers fly in, make a lot of noise, dump on everyone, and then fly out" (p. 38). You can set your expectations and nonnegotiables, but you also have to put supports in place that help those struggling to meet the expectations. Through this Four-Question Model, you are building community and collaboration.

Fullan talks about organizations that value inside collaboration in his *Change Forces: The Sequel* (1999). He notes that you need diversity to prevent "going with only like-minded innovators." He also states that "on the community-building side, these schools and organizations know that the quality of relationships is central to success. Success is only possible if organizational members develop trust and compassion for each other" (p. 37).

Nonnegotiables must be made clear and evident to all stakeholders. For example, if you expect all decisions to be made based on what is best for students (IAK), then that must be a nonnegotiable. As district leader, you must inspect what you expect and make sure that nonnegotiables are being modeled at the school level.

## A Practitioner's Story

Dr. Carmen Coleman, chief academic officer with Jefferson County Public Schools, shared her firsthand experience using the Four-Question Model.

> I will never forget being named superintendent. The feeling was one of tremendous excitement followed by a sense of responsibility almost impossible to describe.
>
> Taking chances and tackling challenges weren't new to me. I already had the opportunity to open a brand new

elementary school as principal. From choosing the paint colors to hiring the staff, I was starting from the ground up in every way. It seemed natural that I would simply paint a clear picture of my vision for the school for those who applied, and then let them decide if they wanted to become a part.

As challenging as it was to open a new school, it paled in comparison to becoming superintendent in a district long steeped in tradition—one whose superintendent vacancy was result of new board members and a new vision—a vision not shared or even understood by everyone in the district and community.

Fortunately, I had a one-of-a-kind mentor who shared the Four-Question Model. He had come into a district long plagued by controversy and negative headlines and had quickly tamed the turbulence. I watched this first from the outside. I was still principal in a neighboring district, and I remember being just in awe of the change I could see in headlines and news stories. It was like he had a Midas touch!

A short time later, I learned that the superintendent had placed tremendous value on taking time to ask four questions:

1. What is working (things you do *not* want to change)?
2. What needs to be changed to make this a better place for kids?
3. What needs to be changed to make this a better place for adults?
4. What can I do, as your leader, to do a better job?

He asked, he listened, and he shared the feedback with everyone. I was fortunate enough to join his team shortly after he arrived, and I got to experience firsthand the impact of this important step. Although requiring a tremendous investment of time, the process was simple.

I knew exactly what I would do during my first weeks as superintendent.

I will never forget the reaction from the staff member who I asked to help schedule these sessions. I wanted to start with every person in the district office, every principal, and groups of teachers and students. I asked her to schedule individual meetings. Although she was nothing but professional and eager to help, I know she was thinking, "She's never going to have time to do this."

I met, I asked, and I listened, just as I knew that superintendent had done. I still remember many of the responses I heard and the insights I gained. Afterward, I shared the feedback I had received, and together, we determined important next steps.

Looking back, I realize even more the impact of taking time to ask those four simple questions. Certainly, the insights I gained as a superintendent were invaluable for me as I began to form a plan. I learned so much from each person, important lessons that otherwise might have been learned only in time; and potentially by making mistakes that could have impeded the important work we needed to do for kids.

I also realize, however, that the seemingly simple act of making time for each person and really listening to what they had to say sent a strong message about what I valued: open communication; the perspective of every person, regardless of position or role; transparency, trust, and collaboration.

In that small Kentucky district, we were able, in five years, to make tremendous gains in student achievement. Our college and career readiness rate, for example, more than doubled, and the district moved from a state ranking of 110 to 24.

We were also able to work toward a very different kind of experience for our students—one that required all students to do internships, performance assessments, and ensure a postsecondary plan was well underway before graduation. We were recognized by PBS's *NewsHour*, the *Harvard Letter*, *Getting Smart*, and others for the work we were doing.

I am positive that none of this would have been possible, especially under the circumstances in which I was hired, had I not begun with those four simple questions.

## Clearly Document the Process

Leithwood et al. (2004) conducted a research review for the Wallace Foundation to examine successful district leadership practices that positively impact teaching and learning. The report calls for additional research on how leaders can engage stakeholder groups. The following excerpt outlines the authors' recommendation for further research.

> Such a framework focuses future research on such questions as:
>
> - How do leaders engage those outside the formal institutional structure (parents, community groups, businesses, media and others) in effectively supporting improved teaching and learning? What opportunities for engagement or agenda setting are overlooked or mismanaged?
> - What barriers or opportunities do these stakeholders present? In particular, how do external stakeholders affect the opportunities for school leaders to define broader and more compelling visions for public education and to generate new solutions?
> - How can their role be leveraged to improve students' learning? What strategies do superintendents and principals use to increase democratic participation in the educational enterprise? (Leithwood et al., 2004, p. 50)

## TO SUM UP

This book provides a strategic approach for district leaders to engage stakeholder focus groups. Using the Four-Question Model, district leaders can create a more compelling vision and generate new solutions to barriers in school turnaround while increasing democratic participation in the educational system. School improvement or school turnaround is not always about top-down or grassroots effort—it's about asking and answering questions together—the right questions!

## REFLECTIVE QUESTIONS AND ACTIVITIES

Suggestions on how to use these reflective questions and activities: Focus Group, Professional Learning Community, District Leadership Team Book Study, or Vertical Leadership Teamwork.

You can answer the questions individually or assign questions and then reconvene as a group to review responses. You might also consider using the Think-a-Thon strategy outlined in the Appendix if you want to come together after reading and answer the questions as a group.

1. As district leaders, in what ways are you already modeling vulnerability?
2. In what ways do you demonstrate visionary leadership? Relational leadership?
3. Create a list of stakeholder groups and a focus-group meeting schedule.
4. Compile a list of stakeholders already engaged, and identify the forum or process for their input. How is this

feedback integrated into the district improvement or turnaround plan?
5. Design or revise a clear communication plan that includes the Four-Question Model.

# *Appendix*

# Whole-Group Debriefing Strategy

## THINK-A-THON

### What Is a Think-a-thon?

When you bring together a focus group of knowledgeable and compassionate people, you can capture their diverse perspectives through a Think-a-Thon strategy. This allows participants to start off in a small-group and wrap up the meeting with a whole-group perspective—sharing innovative ways to tackle tough issues or barriers in educational improvement.

### Materials Needed

Four different color markers (dark/bright colors work best)
    Four flip-chart papers with one question written on each flip-chart paper posted in four different corners of the room:
    The four questions are:

1. What is working (things you do *not* want to change)?

2. What needs to be changed to make this a better place for kids?
3. What needs to be changed to make this a better place for adults?
4. What can I do, as your leader, to do a better job?

## Directions

### Step 1

Ask each person in the room to number off from "1" to "4." Then put all of the "1's" next to the first flip chart, which has Question 1 written at the top, "What is working? Things you do *not* want to change."

Ask all of the "2's" to stand beside the flip chart with Question 2: "What needs to be changed to make this a better place for kids?"

The "3's" move to the area beside the flip chart with Question 3: "What needs to be changed to make this a better place for adults?"

Finally, the "4's" stand beside the flip chart with Question 4 written at the top: "What can I do, as your leader, to do a better job?"

### Step 2

Each group identifies a "facilitator" and a "recorder." Give each recorder a different color marker. Tell groups the process will be timed (five minutes each rotation). The facilitator will lead each group by first reading the question at the top of the flip chart paper. Their job is to also make sure everyone participates.

The recorder will jot down as many ideas as they have time to brainstorm in five minutes.

## Step 3

Call time after five minutes; ask groups to rotate clockwise to the next flip chart. They will wait for you to say, "Ready, set, go" before starting each round. At the start of each round, the facilitator reads the previous groups' responses. If there is a response that they agree with, they place a check mark beside that statement. Then they use the remainder of their time to brainstorm new ideas.

This process is conducted a total of four times.

## Step 4

After the fourth and last rotation, teams move back to their original flip chart where the facilitator reviews the overall results. Team members decide if they want to place a check mark beside any new items below their original list.

Each team identifies those items with the highest number of check marks. Give each team about ten minutes to complete this task.

Starting with the "Team 1," the facilitator shares with the whole group what items had the most check marks, which represents the consensus of the focus group. Allow about five minutes for each team facilitator to share.

Ask a district leadership team member to take notes of any conversation in the process that is not captured on the flip charts.

*Step 5*

Wrap up the meeting with an opportunity for questions and answers and any "aha" moments you or group members may have had during the process.

*Step 6*

Take the flip charts back and create a Word document for the results so the data can be analyzed and compared to individual survey results.

# Works Cited

Amabile, Teresa, and Steven J. Kramer. 2011. "The Power of Small Wins." *Harvard Business Review*, May. https://hbr.org/2011/05/the-power-of-small-wins.

Barkley, Stephen G., and Terri Bianco. 2011. *Instructional Coaching with the End in Mind.* New York, NY: Worthy Shorts, Inc.

Berger, Warren. 2014. *A More Beautiful Question. The Power of Inquiry to Spark Breakthrough Ideas.* New York, NY: Bloomsbury.

Blanchard, Ken, Patricia Zigarmi, and Drea Zigarmi. 2000. *Leadership and the One Minute Manager.* New York, NY: HarperCollins Publishers.

Buckingham, Marcus, and Curt Coffman. 2008. *First Break All the Rules: What the World's Greatest Managers Do Differently.* New York, NY: Simon & Schuster.

Daggett, Willard R., and Susan A. Gendron. n.d. *What's Your School's DNA? Using Data to Drive Innovation.* New York, NY: International Center for Leadership Education.

Daly, Alan J. (2010). *Social Network Theory and Educational Change.* Cambridge, MA: Harvard Education Press.

Donohoo, Jenni, John Hattie, and Rachel Eells. 2018. "The Power of Collective Efficacy." *Educational Leadership*, 75(6), 40–44.

Dufour, Richard, and Robert J. Marzano. 2011. *Leaders of Learning: How District, School, and Classroom Leaders Improve Student Achievement.* Bloomington, IN: Solution Tree Press.

Evans, Robert. 1996. *The Human Side of School Change: Reform, Resistance and the Real-Life Problems of Innovation.* San Francisco, CA: Jossey-Bass.

# Works Cited

Fullan, Michael. 1999. *Change Forces: The Sequel.* New York, NY: Routledge.

———. 2001. *Leading in a Culture of Change.* San Francisco, CA: Jossey-Bass.

Gruenert, Steve, and Todd Whitaker. (2015). *School Culture Rewired: How to Define, Assess, and Transform It.* Alexandria, VA: ASCD.

Huseman, Richard, and Merwyn Hayes. (2001). *Give-to-Get Leadership: The Secret of the Hidden Paycheck.* Equity Press.

Kallick, Bena, and Allison Zmuda. 2017. *Students at the Center: Personalized Learning with Habits in Mind.* Alexandria, VA: ASCD.

Kegan, Robert, and Lisa Lahey. 2001. *How the Way We Talk Can Change the Way We Work.* San Francisco, CA: Jossey-Bass.

Leithwood, Kenneth, Karen Seashore Louis, Stephen Anderson, and Kyla Wahlstrom. 2004. *How Leadership Influences Student Learning: A Review of Research for the Learning from Leadership Project.* New York, NY: The Wallace Foundation.

Maxwell, John C. 2013. "Teamwork and Vision Go Hand in Hand." *John C. Maxwell,* March 26. http://www.johnmaxwell.com/blog/teamwork-and-vision-go-hand-in-hand.

Ponterfract, Dan. 2013. *Flat Army: Creating a Connected and Engaged Organization.* San Francisco, CA: Jossey-Bass.

Quinn, Robert E., Katherine Heynoski, Mike Thomas, and Gretchen Spreitzer. 2014. *The Best Teacher in You: How to Accelerate Learning and Change Lives.* San Francisco, CA: Berrett-Koehler Publishers, Inc.

Reeves, Douglas. 2006a. "Leading to Change/Pull the Weeds Before You Plant the Flowers." *Educational Leadership,* 64(1), 89–90.

———. 2006b. *The Learning Leader: How to focus school improvement for better results.* Alexandria, VA: ASCD.

———. 2009. *Leading Change in Your School: How to Conquer Myths, Build Commitment, and Get Results.* Alexandria, VA: ASCD.

Senge, Peter, Nelda Cambron-McCabe, Timothy Lucas, Bryan Smith, Janis Dutton, and Art Kleiner. 2000. *Schools That Learn: A Fifth Discipline Fieldbook for Educators, Parents, and Everyone Who Cares about Education.* New York, NY: Doubleday.

Josh Shipp. "The Power of One Caring Adult." https://joshshipp.com/one-caring-adult/.

Wheatley, Margaret J., and Kellner-Rogers, Myron. 1996. *A Simpler Way.* San Francisco, CA: Berrett-Koehler Publishers, Inc.

Wheatley, Margaret J. 2006. "Relationships: The Basic Building Blocks of Life." *Margaret Wheatley.* http://www.margaretwheatley.com/articles/relationships.html.

Whitaker, Todd. 2012. *What Great Principals Do Differently*. New York, NY: Routledge.
Willink, Jocko, and Leif Babin. 2015. *Extreme Ownership: How US Navy Seals LEAD and WIN*. New York, NY: St. Martin's Press.
Wiseman, Liz. 2010. *Multipliers: How the Best Leaders Make Everyone Smarter*. New York, NY: HarperCollins.

# About the Authors

Stu Silberman and Gay Burden worked together in a Kentucky school district where Stu was the superintendent and Gay was a teacher-leader. Silberman implemented this Four-Question Model in the district, and he was recognized multiple times for his leadership success in district and school turnaround, including being selected as a Final-Four National Superintendent of the Year. Additionally, he was named Kentucky's top superintendent an unprecedented three times. Silberman went on to lead the second-largest school district in Kentucky and then the Prichard Committee for Academic Excellence in Kentucky.

Burden excelled as a teacher-leader and received multiple teaching awards, including the Freedom Foundation's prestigious Leavey Award for Excellence in Free Enterprise Education. She went on to earn a PhD in Curriculum and Instruction and held roles at the district and state levels. She also served as Director of State Services with the Southern Regional Education Board and presently consults with districts across the country in school turnaround and education reform.

As school, district, and state education leaders, Silberman and Burden both understand the importance of asking the right questions to determine a district's DNA. Furthermore, they understand how stakeholder feedback can be used to create a collective vision grounded in their belief that it's about kids.

You can share your own experiences in implementing this model with Stu and Gay by emailing them at askingtherightquestionsbook@gmail.com. They welcome any questions you may have about implementing this model and are available to provide training on the Four-Question Model outlined in this book.

www.ingramcontent.com/pod-product-compliance
Lightning Source LLC
Chambersburg PA
CBHW031643170426
43195CB00035B/566